UNSU

A Story About One Man's
Profound Discovery

www.UNSUBSCRIBE4SUCCESS.com

Editor: Nancy Casey

Printed by

Acknowledgements

I am deeply grateful for my loving and supportive family and friend for their unwavering support during the writing of this book.

Table of Contents

Chapter 1

In Flight

"Keith, congratulations on your promotion! Oh, and that other small thing….saving the company!" said Mr. Wallace, a little out of breath as he walked up to give Keith a hearty handshake.

Keith smiled as he extended his hand to greet his boss. He had been waiting for Mr. Wallace to join him at the gate, and Mr. Wallace was just in time.

Never had Keith dreamed he would be flying internationally for Bibb's Printing Company. Less than a year ago, Bibb's was struggling, but now with the recent changes, the business was not only growing, it was headed for huge success.

Just then, Mr. Wallace's cellphone rang. "Hi, Mr. Schmitt. Looks like our flight is right on schedule."

As his boss continued his conversation, Keith looked over to check the time on the screen. Their flight was about to board.

Before long, Keith and Mr. Wallace were settled on the plane. Mr. Wallace had the window seat, and Keith had the middle seat. Just as Keith started to wonder if the aisle seat would be vacant next to him, a man set his briefcase on the seat and stowed his carry-on in the overhead bin. The man looked at Keith with a big smile and said, "Hello, I'm David."

Keith gave a warm smile. "Hi, I'm Keith."

"Where are you guys headed?" asked David as he buckled into his seat.

"Ruhr, Germany to pick out a custom 3-D printer," Keith told him.

"Oh, wow. That's cool," said David as he settled in for the flight. "Hey, I couldn't help but overhear you and your co-worker talking in the terminal. Did I hear him say you saved your company?"

Before Keith could answer, Mr. Wallace leaned forward and turned to David with a big smile. "He sure did. Our business was headed for disaster until Keith here helped bring about a big change."

"That's great. Do you mind if I ask you what you did? The company I'm working for is really struggling, and we may have to close our doors. We have a long flight ahead of us, and I would love to hear, if you don't mind sharing," said David.

"Well, sure. It's actually quite simple. It all began at home, but quickly got put to use at work," said Keith. "And it won't take much time to tell. I'll start at the beginning."

Chapter 2

What Is It?

"Ever since my wife, Beth, and I got married, there has been a honey-do list posted on our fridge. I had always been good at keeping up with the list of chores, but, after a couple months, I found that I had seriously drifted behind. Almost every time I looked at the list I felt overwhelmed, discouraged, and even a bit upset that I wasn't meeting the needs of my family by helping out. Work had begun to consume my life as it has a tendency to do with most people. As a result, my family life began to suffer.

"One Saturday morning, I finally had a little free time and decided to tackle one of the many projects on the honey-do list. As I looked over the list, I saw that Beth had written and underlined Unsubscribe to junk mail.

"When I saw that… I almost lost it! *I don't have time for this,* I thought. *What an utter waste of my time. Can't we just keep throwing it away every time it comes?*

"Instead I decided to begin by doing something else on the list, something that was easier and quicker, like fix the screen door that had popped off the tracks. As I was re-installing the door for what seemed like the millionth time, it dawned on me that I just needed to make a simple height adjustment to the wheels to fix the problem for once and for all.

"I was so proud of myself for fixing that door. I could not believe it was that easy. If I had made this slight adjustment years ago, I would not have had this continuously showing up on my to-do list and consuming my time.

"I soon wondered what else on the list I could cross off that was reoccurring. Again, my eyes focused on the *Unsubscribe to junk mail.*

5

"I thought, *Well, if I unsubscribe to these catalogs, it will certainly save us a lot of time sorting the mail in the future.*

"I also thought about how my kids had recently started talking more about recycling and the importance of being more 'Earth conscious.'

"I picked up the phone and started calling the various catalogs and unsubscribing. I must say, it took less time than I thought it would. Before long, I had unsubscribed to well over a dozen catalogs and advertisements. One ad did not have a phone number but rather a website I had to go to in order to unsubscribe.

"As I walked into my home office and waited for the computer to boot up, I looked more closely at the advertisement. It was for a basement sealer for making your basement dry. I had looked into this product about five years ago and had requested information on it but never ordered it. It ended up that all I had needed to do in order to fix our wet basement was to add a gutter on the side of the house. I had gone ahead and installed the gutter, which had fixed the problem. Here, five years later, I was still getting advertisements for something that was no longer relevant.

"After I unsubscribed to the basement sealer, I leaned back in my chair wondering what to tackle next on the list. I saw a note I had written reminding myself to print a concert ticket that I had purchased. The concert was a heavy metal band I used to listen to when I was younger. They were going to be in the area next week. I had invited Beth, but she was not interested in going and didn't care for that kind of music.

"As I scrolled through my emails looking for the e-ticket, I started to become frustrated. I couldn't find the email. When I looked more closely at each subject line, I realized that most of my inbox was filled not with personal emails, but with advertisements from different stores and places I had gone, as well as places I had never even heard of. I wondered how I had gotten on so many lists. It was ridiculous!"

David laughed, "Oh man, I have the same problem. I can't stand junk email!"

Just then they were interrupted by a loud announcement from the pilot saying they were ready for take-off. A few moments later they were airborne and David asked, "So did you get rid of all that junk email?"

Keith continued, "Well, it was worse than all the physical junk mail we had been getting in our mailbox that I'd just finished unsubscribing to.

"At first, I just started deleting them. Then I realized that more would just end up back in my inbox in a few days if I didn't unsubscribe to each one. Initially it felt like a huge task, but I opened each email, scrolled to the bottom and moved the mouse to click *unsubscribe*.

"After I finished unsubscribing to all those emails, I realized how much better I felt knowing that I wouldn't have to deal with the same old junk mail anymore. It reminded me of when I was a little boy out weeding in the garden. I quickly discovered that if I didn't pull the weeds up by their roots, they would keep coming back.

"Finally, I found the email for the concert ticket. As I sat there looking at it, I realized that part of me really wasn't interested in going. I was somewhat surprised, because years ago I had missed the concert, and I was deeply disappointed. Now the band was coming to my home town, and I didn't even really want to go. I tried to remember some of the songs they sung. A few of them came to mind, but most I had forgotten.

"I thought about returning my ticket for a refund but discovered that it was non-refundable. I wasn't sure what to do. It felt like a waste of money to abandon the ticket, but after thinking about it further, I realized that the real waste would be to spend time doing something that I didn't want to do. Then I remembered that one of my co-workers had wanted to go but had missed out on the ticket sale. He was a young guy and loved the band. I thought that maybe he'd like to buy my ticket.

"It ended up that I was able to sell the ticket to my co-worker. It was a real win-win. I was able to get out from feeling obligated to go to a concert I did not want to go to, and my co-worker was thrilled to get the ticket.

"Anyway, that night, after Beth and I tucked in the kids, I paid a few bills and then went upstairs to bed. On my way up, I stubbed my toe on a bunch of toys scattered in the hallway. I looked around me, stuff was everywhere. In a moment of frustration a feeling of anger welled up inside of me. I felt suffocated in my own home. I thought to myself, *Do we really need all this stuff? Do we use it? Can't we get rid of some of these toys?*

"That sounds familiar," David interjected. "That frustrates me as well. The stuff really starts to add up fast."

Nodding in agreement, Keith continued.

"When I went into our bedroom, I found that Beth was already asleep. I was a little disappointed, as I was hoping to talk with her but I couldn't blame her for going to bed early. She was always exhausted from all the activities and sports she organized with the kids, and now, being pregnant with our third child, she really needed the extra rest.

"As I lay in bed, I started thinking about how unhappy I had become. I felt stressed at work. The company had been going through a tough time. Family life was suffering, and it was clear that none of us were very happy. I wondered what could change so that I...*we* could have a better life? Needless to say, it was a restless night."

Chapter 3

Aha

"The next morning when I woke up, I noticed how quiet the house was. Everyone was still sleeping. The only sound I could hear was the ticking of my grandfather's pocket watch that lay on the nearby dresser. I had just come across it a few days earlier when I was searching through my nightstand for something. I began thinking about my grandfather. He was an amazing man - very wise, yet he lived so simply. People would often go to him for advice.

"As I lay there wishing he was still around to give me some of his pearls of wisdom, I recalled something he had once shared with me. He said, 'Everyone has the same amount of time each day. It's what we choose to do with it that's important.'

"With that thought, I decided to do something new and different. Instead of staying in bed and going back to sleep, I wanted to surprise my family with homemade French toast. I quietly crept downstairs.

"When I got to the kitchen, I stopped in my tracks. It was a mess! Dirty dishes were stacked on both sides of the sink, backpacks were piled on the kitchen table, and the countertop was cluttered with stuff."

David reached over and lightheartedly nudged Keith's arm. "Sounds like my house!" he said winking.

"So, feeling somewhat discouraged," Keith continue, "I pushed the pots and pans to one side to make some room. As I grabbed the fridge door handle to get the eggs, my eyes fell on the honey-do list. I had forgotten to cross off Unsubscribe to junk mail.

"I opened our junk drawer and searched through the clutter for a pen. I found half of a pencil and began to cross off the completed task. As I did this, I mumbled to myself, 'I wish I could unsubscribe to some of these dirty dishes or the mess on the kitchen table!'

"At that instant, I had an aha moment. Something in me clicked. I realized that just as I had unsubscribed to the junk mail, I could unsubscribe to anything else that I didn't want in my life. It made me wonder what else I should unsubscribe to that wasn't working."

Keith's story was interrupted with the pilot's announcement of beautiful weather ahead for a smooth flight, and that soon the in-flight service would begin.

When the announcement finished, David turned to Keith and said, "That's a brilliant thought! I've never thought of just 'unsubscribing' to what isn't working in your life. So what happened next?"

With a warm smile Keith resumed his story.

"So in spite of the messy kitchen, I still wanted to make French toast for my family. As I reached into the fridge for the eggs, I was surprised by a voice behind me. It was Beth saying that she was glad to see from looking at the list on the fridge door that I'd unsubscribed to the junk mail. I could tell she was relieved that we would have less mail to sort through in the future. I told her she had no idea how good it felt.

"As I made French toast and Beth started to clean up the kitchen, I shared with her the inspiration that came to me just moments before. I talked to her about how maybe we could start simplifying our lives by looking at things we no longer wanted or needed and we could simply Unsubscribe to them. She liked the idea a lot!

"Beth said that she had been feeling overwhelmed lately and that maybe getting rid of some of the clutter would help her start to feel better.

" 'Look around at all this stuff,' she said pointing to some old cords that were tangled up and sitting on the kitchen counter. 'More than half of it we don't even use.'

"Seeing that the cords were mine, I got a little defensive. They belonged to my old work phone. As I began to think about it more, I realized that the cords she had pointed out were outdated. For some reason, I had been holding on to them, and I didn't even know why.

"Now looking back, I see it was out of habit. We all do it. When you have something that was once useful, you hold on to it. It feels like common sense, right? You think it still has value and could be useful in the future, when, in fact, it is obsolete. The funny thing is that many of us go about blindly accumulating what we feel is a wealth of stuff when, in fact, it's just a heavy anchor weighing us down.

"I apologized to Beth for overreacting about the cords. She told me it was okay, and she forgave me.

"As we worked together in the kitchen, we talked more about the idea of Unsubscribing. I suggested that we first come up with a list of what we had been subscribing to. Then we could re-evaluate those things to see what we could let go of.

"Beth had a great example. She brought up our family gym membership that we had been carrying for the last eight months. We always intended to go but never did. We were holding on to it, paying seventy-five dollars each month, with the thought we might go. But we could never seem to find, or make, the time.

"So at what point do you Unsubscribe? At what point should we come to terms with the fact that we just aren't going to go? If we really did end up wanting to go, we could just subscribe again. Meanwhile, we were wasting that seventy-five dollars each month and feeling guilty. Both the wasted money and guilty feelings were things that we were subscribing to without even being aware.

"Anyway, before long, the smell of homemade French toast had lured the kids down to the kitchen. They were so excited to see what was cooking.

"Sadly, it had been over a year since I had made them French toast. We had somehow moved entirely to frozen or pre-packaged breakfasts, you know, to save time and all. But it was sort of funny because I was surprised at how quickly *real* French toast could be made. I had built it up in my mind as being such a time-consuming task. It no longer felt like a task. It was enjoyable!

"It was a great breakfast. We had strawberry topping, whipped cream...the whole nine yards. It was a huge hit.

"After breakfast, my kids asked what was the special occasion for a homemade breakfast. I chuckled and decided this could be the perfect moment to share what I had just discovered. My hope was that they could benefit from it too.

"I told the kids it was time that we all made a change in the family. My dear little daughter looked panicked and blurted out, 'You and mom aren't getting a divorce, are you?'

"I told them absolutely not. Then my son asked if we were moving, saying he didn't want to move away from friends in the neighborhood. I told them, 'No, we aren't moving.' Before they could continue guessing, I told them about my idea of Unsubscribing to clutter and subscribing to more family time. The kids liked the idea.

"My son asked, 'Can we Unsubscribe from cleaning our rooms?'

"My wife piped up saying, 'Not exactly, but how about if we could subscribe to a new way of thinking about how we clean our rooms.'

"Then I suggested that we could each start to look at the things in our lives and decide whether we wanted to continue to subscribe to them or not.

"With this fresh new start, I was looking forward to doing something different that weekend. Our normal routine was to mow the lawn and do chores, and we never deviated from that. It had not rained for a while, and the grass had hardly grown. The house was a mess, but I decided to suggest a change to our routine.

"I asked everyone what they thought about going on a hike down to Pine Beach. The kids loved the idea. I'm sure it was partly because it would get them out of doing chores, but also because they loved the hikes we used to take.

"Beth was hesitant because she was worried that the house would remain a mess all week if we didn't take time to clean it then. She felt that we needed to stick to the schedule.

" 'We always mow the lawn on Sunday,' she said. I told her to look at the lawn. It had hardly grown. Still she was unsure. It can sometimes feel hard to change from a routine."

With a laugh, David said, "I'm not sure I could convince my wife to break that kind of routine. It's really hard when you're working all week and the weekends are the only time available to get things done. So did Beth go for it?"

"When I told her that we could bring a picnic and talk like old times and that we could clean up when we got back, she smiled and said that sounded really nice. She said that maybe we could *subscribe* to the idea that fresh air and exercise would be a welcome change. We both laughed, and with an enthusiastic yell, Beth said, 'Kids, go change out of your pjs. We are going to the beach!'

"The walk was great! The kids played by the shoreline collecting shells and beach glass. Together we built a giant turtle out of sand. Beth and I had great conversations like we used to have, and we talked about what it would be like once we were outnumbered with three kids!

"That afternoon when we returned home, we started to pick up the house. It felt like there was new energy and excitement in the house. It was something I wanted to keep and not lose. At this point, I had no idea how much our lives would be changing for the better.

"That evening, the kids asked if we could do something fun as a family the next weekend as well. I told them maybe we could start taking the time to do more family activities. It made me think again about what my grandfather had said about the importance of how we spend our time.

"After dinner, as we all continued to clean up the house, I started to think again about all the *stuff* we had. The bin of toys that was dumped on the living room floor mostly contained toys that were not even played with anymore. We had four big throw blankets. At most, two were ever in use. The more I looked around, the more I realized that we had a lot of things we no longer used. These *things* were taking up space and also taking up our time as we had to clean, care for, and organize them.

"The infant bouncy seat was a prime example. Our youngest child was five and had outgrown it years ago. I couldn't believe it had sat there five years and I hadn't even noticed it. Soon we would be using it again, but after this next and last child, I decided I would make sure to give it away, rather than store it unnoticed in the corner.

"I asked my kids if they wanted to get rid of some of their toys, and they declined. Then I asked if they enjoyed picking up and keeping track of all the toys. Both kids said it was not much fun. When asked which ones they played with, the kids came up with a very small number. I suggested that we keep only the toys that they were likely to play with and get rid of the rest. That way, clean up would go much quicker, and we would have more time to do other things like have more family outings.

"Suddenly, the simplicity of fewer toys made sense to them. Beth liked the idea as well. With another baby on the way, she felt that anything we could do to make things simpler would be really helpful.

"Before long, it was as if our house had started to transform. We realized how much lighter we felt and how much more inspiring our house looked. We put all the unwanted items into bags and piled them into the garage. I dropped them off at a local charity on my way to work early Monday morning."

"Excuse me," interrupted the flight attendant, offering drinks and pretzels. Refreshed, the two men resumed their conversation.

"That's wonderful you donated your stuff to a charity so people in need could actually put some of that stuff to use," David said.

"Exactly!" Keith agreed. "So after we had simplified our life some by letting go of stuff, Beth and I started wondering how else we could use the Unsubscribe approach. It turned into a lot of fun! The more we used it, the easier life got. Something magical started to happen. We all began to feel happier and closer as a family. Our home was more orderly. We could find what we were looking for much faster and had more time with each other. We even started doing family movie nights each weekend. That had not happened in a long time."

David interrupted, "Wow! Sounds like your family really changed very quickly. I wish I had more time with my kids.

"Maybe you will," said Keith.

"Things are so much clearer now that I view everything as a subscription. I think of all the unnecessary things that I've put myself through because I didn't see that I had a choice and that I was the one choosing."

"Y'know, that's a great point," said David. "Not only can I use this, but my sister could really use this too. She is always complaining about how busy and unhappy she is. Maybe if she knew that she was in charge of her own subscriptions, she could change her life for the better. This seems very practical."

Nodding his agreement, Keith continued, "I think it's very common to think that we're just along for the ride and there isn't much we can do about it. But realizing that you can Unsubscribe to the things in your life that are not serving you is very empowering. Nowadays, I don't waste as much time, or money, subscribing to things that I don't really want or need, both personally and professionally."

Chapter 4

Work Changes

"How does all this relate to your company?" asked David.

"That's exactly what I wanted to share with you next," said Keith. "So before long, I decided I would see if there were ways I could Unsubscribe at work in order to recreate some of the freedom that I was starting to feel at home. I thought maybe I could increase my productivity and focus on the more important tasks. Perhaps I could even get a raise or a promotion in the future if I started to change how I approached certain aspects of my work."

David nodded approvingly. "How'd you even know where to start?"

"Well, I realized I had a tendency to let myself get roped into the gossip that took place in the coffee room all too often. In some ways, it was mildly addictive, but in other ways, perhaps it was just a bad habit. I never felt good after partaking in it, as it always involved putting people down. Usually it was about the people in our neighboring department.

"Seeing the gossip as unproductive, I decided that it would be something to Unsubscribe to.

"That day when I walked into the coffee room, three or four people were gabbing about one of the other office workers. It was somewhat tempting to join in the negative dialogue, as it was an office worker I did not particularly care for. Someone even asked what I thought about this person.

"Just when I was about to respond, I caught myself and decided to Unsubscribe to the gossip. I smiled, grabbed a cup of coffee, and said that I needed to get back to work. As I sat down at my desk,

I remember thinking how liberating it felt not to have partaken in it.

"As fate would have it, a few minutes later, the office worker who'd been gossiped about walked over to my desk and said that he appreciated the report I had put together the week before. I thanked him, and we talked for a few minutes, and then he left.

"I know that had I been gossiping about him prior to him coming over, I would have felt pretty bad inside. I would have mulled over the interaction in my head for a few minutes, which would have led to even less productivity."

"I would have done the same thing," said David. "I'm always rehashing conversations in my head in situations like that. Go on. I want to hear more."

Keith continued, "Over the course of a couple weeks, I found even more ways in which I could Unsubscribe. Next, I de-cluttered my desk. Now, with a clean desk, I can find things much quicker, which saves me a few minutes each day since I no longer have to waste time looking for things. I did the math and it turns out that an organized desk saves me at least thirty minutes each week.

"As I started Unsubscribing to things that no longer applied or that I had outgrown, I found that I had more time to focus on what was important.

"Before long I was able to get all my work done much more efficiently. When a special project came up and I had to work longer hours to get it done it was much more manageable. This was due to having Unsubscribed from all the things that had been keeping me from being as productive.

"Overall, I can work more normal hours. With this newfound free time, I'm able to spend more time with my family or do an activity that sparks my interest like playing my guitar which up until recently I had not played for years.

"The idea of Unsubscribing came at a perfect time for me. My life had been unraveling, and I had absolutely no clue how to fix it. My relationship with Beth and the kids had been going down the tubes, work was always bogging me down, and it looked like I would never be able to move up the corporate ladder. This, along with having a third child on the way, had me feeling helpless."

The two men sipped their drinks thoughtfully.

David spoke up, "This actually sounds like a lot of people I know. I'm really glad you're sharing this story with me. It's coming at the perfect time. So what happened next?"

"After a few months of streamlining things at work, I was scheduled to meet with my boss, Mr. Wallace," Keith continued, pointing to the man sitting next to him.

He turned, expecting Mr. Wallace to be listening in on the conversation, but instead found him listening intently to an audio book, *The New One Minute Manager*, with his headset on and writing notes on a yellow notepad.

"I remember the meeting quite well. As I walked into Mr. Wallace's office he told me to take a seat. He stroked his beard and squinted his eyes as he looked across his cluttered desk at me. It was clear that he was deep in thought. I had no clue why I had been called into his office.

"After a long pause, he told me how he had noticed a significant change in me—a change in my performance. He said that he had always admired my work ethic, but this was something quite different. He knew my work load had not changed, yet my efficiency and performance certainly had. He said that it even looked like I was enjoying myself more.

"I told him those things were all true. That's when I shared with him the simple idea of Unsubscribing to things that don't serve you and subscribing to things that do. I told him about how I had started to look at the choices I was making in my life and deciding whether to continue with them or not.

"He asked me to elaborate. I shared with him how I had started to look at everything in my life as a subscription. I had concluded that, for the most part, the things and circumstances around me were all a conglomeration of my choices or, as I was now calling them, my 'subscriptions.'

"I let him know how I loved the idea of looking at things as if they were on a subscription basis. It allowed me to feel like I was empowered and when I looked at things that way, I could change things much more easily and get better results.

"If something or someone no longer fit into my life, whatever the reason was, I could choose to

Unsubscribe and let it, or them, go. I no longer felt shackled to all the things that I had signed up for in the past. I was not bound to old choices or decisions, and there was a way out. I had the freedom at anytime to adopt something new and better to support the direction I was moving in at that moment.

"He was astonished by this, and said that it sounded surprisingly simple yet profound. He asked if that was really all that was behind the shifts that I had made. I assured him it was.

"Then he surprised me by saying that he was going to start using this approach himself."

With a tap on David's shoulder, the flight attendant again apologetically interrupted them but they were glad to see their meals had arrived.

After exchanging jokes about the mystery meat in the meal, David grew serious. "Sounds like your boss was pretty open-minded about Unsubscribing. But did he ever end up using it himself?"

"Well I found out soon enough," Keith replied. "A few weeks later, I was called back into his office. This time when I entered, I saw that his office had been rearranged. The flow seemed to make more sense. The cluttered papers that once sat on his desk were no longer there. Over to the left of the desk were two new filing cabinets.

"He told me that the simple approach of asking yourself what you do and don't want to sign up for had made a big difference to him.

"He said that he'd ended up telling his wife about it, and she also started finding ways to use it. He mentioned that he was supposed to go to an event that past weekend, but did not want to go. When his wife asked him why he was going, he told her that it was because he felt obligated. Apparently it had been tradition to go to this particular event.

"She told him that it was a tradition that he needed to Unsubscribe from as he'd never gotten anything out of it. He said he laughed and told her that she was absolutely right. He told her he would gladly *Unsubscribe* to that!"

"Smart man!" David exclaimed.

"Exactly!" Keith agreed with a laugh. "So then he told me that since he'd observed such a positive change in me and my work, he'd come to the conclusion he should propose something to me.

"I remember how my palms started to sweat as I waited for him to continue. He told me how he would like me to give a short fifteen minute talk on this Unsubscribe approach to all of the employees. He said that if they can't get it in that amount of time, they're not going to get it, so I should keep it simple and brief.

"Suddenly, part of me wished that I hadn't shared the idea with him. I really did not like public speaking. To get up in front of sixty people and talk was not something I did.

"I guess I must have looked a little flushed because Mr. Wallace asked me, 'What's the matter? You look concerned.'

"I decided to open up a little and just tell him that I was great in small groups but large groups intimidated me. He laughed and suggested that I might Unsubscribe to that belief. He said I would do just fine, and that I should plan on giving the presentation next Monday.

"When I left his office, I started to feel anxious about what I would say. Would my co-workers think the idea was stupid?

"That evening after dinner, I talked it over with Beth. She told me the same thing that Mr. Wallace had told me. She suggested I just Unsubscribe to my worry about how it might be received and instead subscribe to the fact that this method works! She reminded me of how our entire family had transformed.

"It felt like the Unsubscribe approach, which had seemed so simple and had been serving me so well, would fail me here. I started to come up with reasons why it wouldn't work in this case.

"You see, I had a history of failed public speaking experiences. When I went to deliver my best man speech at my best friend's wedding it had come out terrible. I had rehearsed the speech about thirty times, yet when I stood up in front of all those people, I felt tongue tied. I stumbled over the carefully written words that I had poured so much thought into. My hands trembled and my voice cracked as I attempted to read from the wrinkled up paper. In my mind, the speech had been a disaster. It had left a scar on me that I had been carrying around for a long time. That was nineteen years ago, but I was still holding on to that moment in time as if it were yesterday.

"Late that evening as I mulled over possible ways that I could try to get out of giving the speech, something suddenly clicked in me.

"Maybe Mr. Wallace and Beth were right. Maybe I could choose to Unsubscribe from the fear that was trying to trap me in an experience that had happened nearly two decades ago.

"The self-condemnation needed to stop. I decided to allow myself to create a new experience by subscribing to a thought I was more worthy of.

"Just thinking that way made me look at things from a different perspective. It occurred to me that I've always been a good storyteller. My kids, who are very upfront and honest, tell me so. You gotta love kids...they hold nothing back. Even my wife often comes in to listen to the bedtime stories that I tell them. On many occasions, she has even marveled over how creative they are.

"It struck me that maybe I could just look at the speech as simply a story that I would be telling. I started to love this new perspective. This was an idea that was worth subscribing to!

"It would be a story about my discovery of how a simple act of Unsubscribing to junk mail ended up changing my life. I thought about how others could take this simple idea and discover ways to start subscribing to things that would better serve them, precisely in the way Mr. Wallace and his wife had made their own discoveries.

"As I thought more about it, the pressure of having to teach or tell someone what to do faded away. All I was doing was sharing a tool. Not one that I created, but rather stumbled across. My co-workers would be the ones that could take this tool, called *Unsubscribe,* and use it in any way that served them.

"Before I knew it, Monday morning had arrived, and I was in the conference room at the podium. My co-workers sat before me. Some, I'm sure, were wondering what I could possibly offer them.

"Initially a little nervous, I shared my story with them, just as I am sharing it with you now. The response was better than I expected. In fact, it was great. Afterwards, several people came up to me and shared ways in which they planned on Unsubscribing. It was wonderful, as there were a number of ideas that I would never have thought of. A few people said that they'd noticed a change in me and had been wondering how it had come about. Some asked me how long it had taken. I told them that as soon as I got the basic concept, I began using it right away. The more I used it, the more ways I discovered how it could be used.

"I told them that I never had to work at it. Once you understand the principle of Unsubscribe, you just find yourself using it in your everyday life. It's a great way to make decisions. It becomes a natural and easy way to approach things. Is this subscription going to serve me? If the answer is no, then don't subscribe.

"Sometimes I find my subscriptions are very temporary. They may serve me for a while, and when they're no longer needed, I simply Unsubscribe.

"It was interesting to see how quickly *Unsubscribe* started to become part of the office language. People were discovering wonderfully effective ways to use it. For some, it became a fun approach to solving various daily situations in the office. In fact," Keith said pulling his phone out of his pocket and bringing up a photo for David to see, "look at this. Someone even changed a poster in our office!"

"TO BE ~~BE~~ Subscribe

OR

~~NOT TO BE~~ Unsubscribe

THAT IS THE QUESTION."

-WILLIAM ~~SHAKESPEARE~~ Keith

They shared a laugh. "After several weeks had gone by," Keith continued, "there was a noticeable difference in the office. It was almost as if the Unsubscribe approach had become somewhat contagious.

"When I had first started working at Bibb's, we used to have hour-long meetings every Monday morning. At these meetings, people would socialize, eat donuts, and drink coffee. Amongst all the socializing, *if* you were paying attention, you might pick up a couple good ideas from co-workers. Although aspects of the meetings were helpful, there was too much that needed to be sorted through in order to get the few valuable ideas that may have been there. At some point, it was almost unanimously decided that it was not worth losing an hour of work time each Monday to get what we got from the meetings. So they were canceled.

"But one thing that got lost in eliminating those meetings was an element of teamwork. Everyone seemed to have their own ideas about things, and now those ideas were rarely shared.

"However, now with the positive shifts in the office, Mr. Wallace decided to institute a shortened version of the regular meetings we once had. He was very interested in learning how people had been applying the Unsubscribe approach in their various departments and felt that sharing this information could be beneficial to everyone.

"Upon hearing that we would be starting up Monday meetings again, several of my co-workers became upset. They did not want to go back to Monday meetings. Some even confronted Mr. Wallace and tried to convince him to keep things the way they were.

"He told them that the meetings would be more like briefings than meetings. They would only be fifteen minutes in length. His idea was to cut out eighty percent of the fluff from the past meetings and just focus on the really valuable insights.

"It ended up being a great idea. The focus was on what people were able to cut out of their days to make them more efficient. There were lots of great suggestions for ways in which we could Unsubscribe as individuals and as a business as a whole.

"At one of the meetings a co-worker named Ted decided to speak up. Ted was our maintenance man. He was relatively shy and stuttered when he spoke. Because of this, some of my co-workers looked down on him. Some even made fun of him.

"I still remember all the heads that turned when Ted began to share that day. He suggested that each week we would pick a topic to Unsubscribe to. This topic would be posted on the office bulletin board, and everyone in the office could focus on ways in which they could Unsubscribe to it.

"I remember seeing a few of my co-workers roll their eyes at the idea. Mr. Wallace was eager for new ideas, so he decided we would try it for a week and see how it went.

"He asked Ted to choose the first topic. Ted paused, looked down, and proceeded to say slowly, 'How about Unsubscribing to gossip?'

"So, later that week, *Unsubscribe to Gossip* was posted on the bulletin board next to the break room. Having just worked through Unsubscribing to gossip myself, I was very aware of how prevalent it was and also how easy it was to take part in it.

"I was amazed to see the transformation that occurred over the course of the week. Many of my co-workers would catch themselves gossiping and quickly change the subject or walk away. It was surprising how many people actively tried to reduce the amount of gossip that they participated in. As I walked around the office at various points throughout my day, it was refreshing to hear very different conversations than what I had heard in previous weeks."

David nodded. "This is encouraging. My wife was just talking about all the gossip where she works and how it affects their efficiency."

Keith added, "I want to say that, although there was a noticeable reduction in the gossip, it was not completely eradicated. In fact, one day while walking over to the drinking fountain to fill my water bottle, I overheard one of my co-workers, the one who was known as the 'gossip queen,' gossiping about the gossipers. She did, however, have a much smaller group around her than she normally did.

"The following week at the Monday briefing, one of my co-workers shared that he had really been focused on not gossiping throughout the week. He said that he was embarrassed by his past behavior. He had reflected on all the times he had gossiped, and it greatly saddened him. He apologized to everyone and vowed to do better in the future.

"As I listened to him, I turned my gaze to the 'gossip queen' who was sitting quietly with her head down. I could tell that she was affected by what he had shared. In the upcoming weeks, even she reduced the amount she gossiped.

"Since then, each week a new topic for the Unsubscribe was posted on the bulletin board. We collectively Unsubscribed to clutter, jealousy, anger, excuses, procrastination, and even things like fear. And nowadays people really look forward to the Monday briefings."

David raised his eyebrows and said, "Based on that list, we sure have a lot to Unsubscribe to in our company. Did you find everyone started using this new approach?"

Keith smiled. "I wish I could say that everyone embraced the Unsubscribe approach, but they didn't. Some people in our office adopted it on day one. Others started using it when they saw the success others were having around them. There are a few co-workers that still have never used it.

"For most of the employees though, it's become their normal way to approach things. People use it because it works and they see results in their lives.

"After about three months of Unsubscribing, a co-worker named Rose suggested that we change the office bulletin board to read *Subscribe* and start focusing on things we could Subscribe to. The idea was a big hit. We'd spent a fair amount of time Unsubscribing to things that didn't serve us, and now it was time to shift the focus to what we might want to Subscribe to, what might serve us better.

"Following Rose's suggestion, one co-worker blurted out, 'How about Subscribing to a raise?' Everyone laughed."

"That must've gone over big with the boss," David joked.

Keith grinned. "In a way, it actually did! Mr. Wallace just said, 'You laugh, but if we start improving and growing this company and the company becomes more profitable, that could be a real possibility.'

"Then he told us how important each one of us was, that we were what really made the company what it is. He said that if we started Subscribing to and coming up with new, successful ideas that we could transform this company. It was a very powerful speech and a pivotal moment for the company. People left the meeting feeling inspired, knowing that they could help shape the company's future and their own.

"For the first time, we really started to feel like a true team, one where we support one another for the greater good and betterment of our company. In all my years of working at Bibb's, we'd never had such an inspirational message from the boss.

"After the briefing, I asked him what had inspired him to speak out like that. He said that he was now Subscribing to a new method of leadership. You see, he'd been groomed and taught by both his grandfather and father that in order to run a successful company you had to use an authoritarian approach. Mr. Wallace never liked this way of doing things because he said it always felt cold and made him feel distant from the employees. Regardless, he had felt it was the only way, at least until he discovered the power of Unsubscribing.

"Sure, he had gotten results using the old way of leadership, but he wanted to try something different. He moved to a leadership role that was more team oriented. He felt he could get better results, and he does.

"The employees feel empowered. As a result, the work environment has become friendlier and more productive.

"This increase in productivity is quite literally paying off for everyone. In fact we were recently told that at the end of this year, we would all be receiving a bonus check that would be based on any increase in sales from those of last year."

"Well that sure is nice," said David.

"No kidding!" said Keith. "This new, more inclusive leadership style has resulted in many new powerful ideas that have propelled us forward. Interestingly, many of these ideas came from people who had not historically been the ones to speak up; people I would never have expected.

"One co-worker, Caroline, pointed out that Bibb's was sitting on one of the most prime pieces of real estate in the city. Over the years, Canal Street, where Bibb's was located, has grown into a high-end banking district. Real estate on this particular block goes for a very high premium. Her suggestion was to sell this valuable building and move three blocks away where real estate is about half the price yet still in a wonderful section of town. Caroline had noticed that there were a couple of large, updated buildings that had recently gone on the market.

"At first, Mr. Wallace was not at all open to the possibility of selling. Bibb's had been started almost a hundred years ago by his great grandfather in that very building, and he did not intend to move it.

"However, after a couple of weeks of thinking about it, Mr. Wallace decided that the idea was a great one. He said that Bibb's needed to change with the times. The majority of our business is now done through the internet and over the phone. Rarely have we had walk-in customers, so occupying such prime real estate had no real advantage any more. Selling the building, which Bibb's owned outright, and purchasing another in a different location would free up capital to grow the business.

"Plus it would solve many of the problems Bibb's was experiencing with that location. You see, as the banking district had developed over time, parking had become extremely difficult to find. The increased traffic had also made it tricky for drivers to back up their trucks to the building.

"So, not long after Mr. Wallace made his decision, the building sold without even having officially gone on the market. An investment bank paid us top dollar, and we were able to purchase a building that was even larger and had a better layout for our purposes. It's just two blocks away from our previous location, and was less than half of the cost.

The new building has two loading docks with plenty of room for trucks to maneuver, and ample parking for the employees. It is wonderful to see how everything worked out.

"It was Unsubscribing to the old location, and Subscribing to a new, better location that eventually made it possible for us to go on this business trip today in search of a 3-D printer. The capital that was freed up from the sale of the building will allow us to buy this printer and help us make many other changes. This new technology will give our business a huge boost."

At that moment, the flight attendants arrived to collect the meal trays. Once the cumbersome service cart passed, David unbuckled his seat belt.

"Excuse me for a moment. Nature calls!" said David.

Keith took the opportunity to stand and stretch for a few moments, thinking about all the changes that had occurred at work.

Chapter 5

Expanding

While his seatmate was away, Keith wondered what David was thinking about the Unsubscribe approach. Would he choose to make changes at work and in his life the way Keith had? Pondering this, Keith looked around. A woman sitting across and up a row from him made eye contact, smiled and gave a slight nod. He noticed that a few other passengers also were looking his way.

A little while later, David returned. As he sat down in his seat, he said, "This is all very encouraging. I like how simple this approach is. You look at your life and decide to Unsubscribe to the things that don't work, and Subscribe to things that do. I wish I had heard of this years ago. It could have saved me a lot of wasted time and energy. Please continue. I'd love to hear more."

Keith smiled. He reached for his glass of sparkling water, took a sip, and then continued.

"You may, or may not, know this but the printing industry has gone through a huge change now that we're living in the digital age. Most printing houses have been struggling, laying people off and going out of business. Many tend to stick to old ways of doing things. At Bibb's, we were no different. That is, up until we started using this new approach.

"If we hadn't Unsubscribed from our old ways in these fast changing times, we wouldn't have survived. Quite frankly, we were headed in the direction of the buggy whip business—obsolete.

"Now, by Subscribing to broader printing markets and new technologies, Bibb's has increased sales dramatically. The employees are more involved and focused on making the company a success.

"As long as we periodically look at what we're Subscribing to and don't over-Subscribe and over-leverage ourselves, we will thrive by doing this."

"Hmm…," pondered David. "I can see how it could be easy to over-Subscribe with lots of new ideas coming in, especially if they are good ones."

"Yes," said Keith. "Initially when we began to receive an influx of great new ideas it created some problems. We started to go in too many directions at once. It didn't take long before we realized that over-Subscribing was not a good thing. Once we recognized what we were doing, we decided that we needed to step back and make more realistic decisions on where and how to expand and change."

"Do people feel stifled if they're encouraged to share their ideas and then their ideas aren't used?" asked David.

"Good question," said Keith. "What we do is re-direct their creativity. We settle on a main idea and then encourage people to help grow that idea. That way people use their creative energy expanding upon and growing specific ideas that we decide to implement.

"A good example was when one of our employees suggested something that clients had been requesting for years: expanding our website to add the ability to take online orders. Even though we had a fairly extensive online presence, we did not offer the customer the ability to approve their own work and place an order without first talking with us. This created some frustration for the clients especially when it came to more basic print jobs like business cards or repeat orders.

"We had lots of excuses for not changing. One excuse was we knew how complex some printing jobs could be and we didn't believe that even simple orders could be entered and completed without involving a human to help with the order.

"Sadly, the request for online shopping capabilities was a recurring one from our customers. We heard them, but at the same time, we didn't. We were not listening. We took no action.

"Now we not only listen and review all comments and feedback, we also do follow up communications asking how we can make the experience even better. We have received a number of great ideas from our customers this way. Several customers have even recently commented on how refreshing it is to have a company that listens and makes changes.

"A number of the suggestions have been small, easy things to do, but they make a huge difference to the customer. One suggestion was emailing a shipping confirmation when the items ship. This was very simple to implement. It saves the customer from having to call and ask when they will be receiving their order. It also saves us time by not having to field these calls.

"Also, for years we'd been sending out free computer mouse pads with our logo printed on them. We recently received feedback that no one wants them. They get thrown away.

"Now we send pens with our name on them. Pens get used more and seem to be much more appreciated. Also, it saves us about forty cents per order. The labor for screen printing the mouse pads added up and was costing us money that we didn't need to spend.

"These are just a couple examples of the numerous new ideas that we've Subscribed to and put into use. It's been fun to see and be a part of a company that is changing and growing in such positive ways."

David commented, "That sure sounds like a place I'd want to work. But earlier I heard you say that there are a few people who haven't wanted to use the Unsubscribe approach for whatever reason. What happens to those folks?"

"I've noticed that those people tend to be the unhappy ones in the office," Keith answered. "There's a noticeable difference in efficiency and quality of life between those who have adopted the Unsubscribe approach and those who have chosen not to adopt it. Many of those who've taken to Unsubscribing have advanced within the company.

"Not long after all the changes were made that I've told you about, I was called into Mr. Wallace's office again. He told me how pleased he was that this simple approach had transformed the business in such a noticeable way. He also said he could foresee that if we started using some of the newer printing technology, we could grow the business even more.

"In the past, he had been resistant to changing to a new system as it would have meant retraining all the employees and buying new, expensive equipment. Now he had Subscribed to a new way of looking at things. He now saw this as a huge opportunity for growth, and an investment in the company and its future. He saw how fast people were changing and adapting, and realized it would not be as hard to switch over to the new technology as he had led himself to believe."

Just then, Mr. Wallace with his headphones dangling from one ear leaned over Keith and chimed in, "This is why I wanted Keith to be my new production manager.

"The former production manager was my nephew, Roy. Years ago, I hired him as a favor to my sister. Unfortunately, Roy always struggled with finding and keeping a job. He wasn't very driven. Also, he was argumentative and insisted on doing things his own way.

"I struggled with this dilemma for years but did nothing about it. As a result my company suffered. We all suffered greatly, in fact. After numerous talks with Roy, I gave up and allowed him to handle the production side of things the way he wanted. This created a lot of tension in the production department. There were always tiffs between Roy and other co-workers.

"After Keith shared Unsubscribe with me, I came to the realization that we could not afford to keep Roy any longer. We needed to Unsubscribe to him. Surprisingly, Roy ended up being somewhat amiable about being let go. I did endure some wrath from my sister, but she soon got over it.

"Roy, as you might suspect, was one of the few at Bibb's who chose not to adapt to all the changes that were taking place. This somewhat expected response made the decision even easier to let Roy go," said Mr. Wallace.

David nodded sympathetically to Mr. Wallace. "That makes good sense." Looking at Keith, he added, "So that's how you ended up getting this position."

"Yes. I was so excited to be offered the position of production manager. It was a dream come true for me," said Keith. "But truthfully, it was a bit overwhelming at first.

"Fortunately for me, Roy had reluctantly agreed to stay on for two weeks in order to give me a crash course on the ins and outs of his days and everything that needed to be done. I found it very interesting as he walked me through his step by step process. In the past, I would have followed every single step I was told because I would have assumed it was the right way to do things. After all, the guy had been with the company for nearly ten years.

"However, now I was armed with the Unsubscribe approach! I could see that there was a lot that could be changed, streamlined, or cut out all together.

"Unsubscribing was the key that unlocked the door to change. It happened at home, and it happened at work. It's never too late to Subscribe to something new and better," Keith added with a smile.

Chapter 6

Overheard

As the head flight attendant made the announcement that the international flight was soon to be landing in Germany, the passengers began to prepare themselves for arrival.

"Wow!" David enthused. "This seemed like a really quick trip! I'm so grateful I got to sit next to you and hear this. I have just been given an amazing tool that I have a great need for. This has the potential to change the company where I work."

"That would be great!" said Keith. "I hope you're able to put it to good use. It's been a game changer for us. And, on a personal note, it's changed my life tremendously."

Keith chuckled and shook his head as he recalled some of the crazy things he had Subscribed to over the years. "I'm grateful to have discovered this. Work and life are much more enjoyable."

"I can imagine," said David with a grin. "I'm already thinking of several things I need to Unsubscribe to right now."

"Good! You may find yourself laughing as you let some of your old subscriptions go," said Keith. "It does become humorous at times, as we discover what we've been holding on to and what we've signed ourselves up for."

David responded, "I'm thinking of work and ways to streamline some of our processes by Unsubscribing to things that we've always done but likely don't need to continue doing.

"I can see this as being powerful. I'm excited about getting back to work and trying this process out. Frankly, I haven't been excited to go to work for over a year now, since things seemed destined for failure. But now maybe this Unsubscribe approach can help us turn around our company as you have with yours."

David leaned back in his chair thinking about how he would apply this new approach to his life. After a few minutes of silence went by, Keith noticed a blond-haired woman turn and look at him from between the seats in front of them.

"Sorry to have been listening in, but what you shared about Unsubscribing is exactly what I needed to hear," said the woman.

"Oh," chuckled Keith. "I'm so glad."

Wanting to engage more in conversation, the woman continued, "It feels like choosing my own Subscription is something that I can easily do."

"It's simple and easy," Keith agreed.

The woman said, "Well, you can bet I will be using this right away. I'm already thinking of things that I can Unsubscribe from and simplify my life."

"That's wonderful," said Keith. "Have fun with it!"

"Well, since others are chiming in, I will say that I too couldn't help but overhear your story," said a woman in a blue suit sitting across the aisle from David. "I'm one of those people that absolutely hates their job. I'm good at it, but I hate it," said the woman emphatically.

"Gee, sounds bad," said David. "What do you do? Are you a tax collector for the IRS or something?" They laughed.

"No," smiled the woman. "Probably worse. I'm a telemarketer. You know, one of those people that calls you at dinner time and talks so fast to try to keep you on the phone and prevents you from getting a word in, so that I can try to sell you something that you probably don't want and certainly don't need, but I am going to try to convince you of it anyway. Look, I'm doing it to you now," laughed the woman.

"Well, after hearing what you said, I may think hard about Unsubscribing to this career all together," said the woman. "I see how it's been hurting me. I am not very pleasant to my family and not happy at all.

"This is not the path I want to be on. I think the only reason I've kept on it is because I'm afraid that I can't find another job. Well, I am going to Unsubscribe to that," said the woman as she threw back her shoulders and held her chin up high.

"Well, if it feels right, then I would go with it," said the man sitting next to her.

David asked Keith for a business card so they could keep in touch. As Keith went to hand him one, a few others asked for one as well. It became quite clear that a number of the nearby passengers had tuned into his story. Some passengers said they wanted to be in contact with Keith to share how they were going to be using Unsubscribe.

One person even asked if they could start an informal email correspondence group. Some people thought it was a good idea, and business cards were exchanged among them.

A man sitting in a row behind Keith muttered loudly enough to be overheard. "Geez you all are kidding yourselves – it's not that easy to change."

David leaned close to Keith, lowered his voice, and said, "Sounds like your former production manager Roy."

"Indeed!" chuckled Mr. Wallace.

As the plane touched down and taxied to the gate, Keith slipped his few remaining business cards into the side pocket of his carry-on and slid the bag's strap over his shoulder. He was just about to turn on his cell phone, but then thought maybe it would be better to be unplugged for a little longer and reflect on all the good that had just happened. He took a deep breath and smiled to himself as he followed the line of people toward the open door of the plane. This had been a productive trip already.

Chapter 7

Remember Me

About two weeks later, Keith received an email with the subject line: "Remember me from the plane?"

It read:

Hi Keith,

I don't know if you remember me, but I sat in front of you on the flight to Germany a couple of weeks ago. I was the business woman with the burgundy hair.

Anyway, you gave my co-worker one of your business cards. I did not get a chance to talk with you directly, but I heard what you shared about unsubscribing and I decided to give it a try.

I shared the idea with my husband, and he liked it. In fact, he suggested that we have a yard sale sometime soon and unsubscribe to the things we no longer needed.

We ended up having one last Saturday. Everything that we sold or gave away we haven't even given another thought to. We hadn't realized how much of a weight these unnecessary items had been. It felt so good to clear them out.

You know, the people that ended up coming to the yard sale were so grateful. It made us realize that by holding on to these *things,* we were actually depriving someone who could really use and enjoy them.

What really made me aware of this was when one lady purchased a toy doll that I had. I never even liked dolls. It had been a gift, and I had held onto it out of obligation. Anyway, a woman picked it up and said she used to have this exact doll. Her mother had given it to her, and it had gotten destroyed in a fire. She was practically in tears when she came up to pay for it. I was so glad that I had decided to let it go.

We estimated that there were between forty and fifty people that walked away with something from the yard sale. That's a lot of people that benefitted!

Now that we have room in our living room, my husband said he would get me a piano. I am thrilled because I have wanted one for years, but we never had the space. I am so excited to start taking lessons!

Thank you for sharing this invaluable approach. I'm having fun unsubscribing to the old and making room for the new!

Best, Cindy

Over the next week or so, Keith received a couple other emails from the passengers who had overheard his story. It was clear that when people heard about Unsubscribe, they were discovering ways to apply it in their own lives. Keith was amazed to hear the ways in which people were using it.

One evening at dinner, Keith printed out and shared with Beth a recent email he had received from a co-worker in the advertising department at Bibb's. The email was quite touching and profound.

Dear Keith,

I wanted to thank you for helping save my marriage. I know you did not save it per se, but in a roundabout way you did.

When you initially introduced the Unsubscribe approach at the office, I must admit I was a bit skeptical. It seemed too easy. I dismissed it. Then I started seeing it used throughout the office. I saw firsthand the positive effects it was having on both my co-workers and the company.

Upon seeing it work for so many people, I decided to give it a shot. For some reason, I had pictured it being something you had to "try" to do. It ended up being just to the contrary. It was easy. In fact, I found that it was easier to unsubscribe than it was to continue subscribing to things that either no longer worked, or that I did not want to participate in.

I knew that Bibb's needed a new approach to its advertising. It always felt like we could not make any changes because the budget was fixed and the funds were always spoken for. Traditionally, we had always advertised in the same places because they'd always worked for us. Sure, I would write new ads and create new graphics each month to make our ads look exciting and fresh, but that seemed to yield little fruit.

It did not take long before it occurred to me that all the various places we advertised were "subscriptions." It felt like, duh…what was I thinking?

Anyways, I realized we did not have to be fixated on advertising with these places. They might have worked and served us in the past, but things had changed. We needed to look at what we were subscribing to and discover new places that worked whether it be online or in a magazine or newspaper.

I took a closer look at the statistics of the places we were advertising, so that I could get a feel for which ones were yielding customers for us. We had done this years ago, and that is how we initially determined who to advertise with. Perhaps these old subscriptions were no longer effective.

The analytics revealed that about half of the places we were advertising with were no longer yielding effective results. I unsubscribed to those and found several new places that were very promising and subscribed to those instead. A number of new clients have resulted from these new subscriptions.

This is all fantastic in itself, but the reason that I am writing is a bit more personal.

My marriage has been on the rocks for several years. My wife and I used to have such a good relationship. We were so in love.

But over the past three years or so, things had changed. Neither of us were happy. We both had concluded that this is just how it was going to be.

After successfully using the Unsubscribe approach at work and seeing how easy and effective it was, I decided that I had nothing to lose by trying it with my marriage.

I thought back to the days when we were so in love and had such good times. What had we subscribed to back then and what were we subscribing to now? I thought about how there must be one or more subscriptions that were hurting us.

At first as I thought about it, I found myself blaming her for how things had become. I soon realized this was getting me nowhere. Then it dawned on me…this is what I do. I blame her. I pretty much blame her for everything.

Somewhere along the line, I subscribed to the need to be right. This was hard for me to swallow. After I digested what I had uncovered, I thought about what I could replace this subscription with. Kindness is what came to mind. I could practice being kind rather than feeling a need to be right.

It was amazing to see the difference. This new subscription had a ripple of beneficial effects. We started to have conversations again rather than brief interactions. I no longer felt the need to raise my voice and overpower her. My blood pressure went down. We were happier. I found that even when I thought I was right, if I gave her a chance to communicate, I heard new perspectives that I would have missed.

Not that it mattered, but I thought back to when I had started to subscribe to the need to be right. It was around the time that our only son went away to college. We were very close. As our son lived with us for eighteen years and then was suddenly gone, I guess a part of me felt lost. He was a four hour flight away, and we rarely saw him anymore.

I think unconsciously that was when I subscribed to the need to be right. It stemmed out of a need to be in control. He had grown up. Since I had lost control of our son, so to speak, I found myself attempting to control my wife through the need to be right. I know it doesn't make much rational sense, but that's where I believe that subscription came from.

The great thing that I have discovered with unsubscribe is that it is simple, and you don't have to know where or how you subscribed to something. If it does not fit, then unsubscribe!

Now that I have replaced the need to be right with being kind, our marriage and relationship have improved tenfold.

I don't always agree with everything my wife says, but I don't have the need or desire to force my beliefs on her anymore.

Since regaining a lot of what we had lost, I have shared the unsubscribe approach with her. Together we've been finding ways, both individually and collectively, to just subscribe to the things that work. We let the rest go.

Our quality of life and marriage has drastically improved. With this new approach things just keep getting better.

Much Gratitude, Bill

As Keith set down the letter next to him on the table, he looked across at Beth. She was smiling. "Who would have ever thought so much inspiration and change could have come from Unsubscribing to junk mail?" she asked.

Keith laughed and said, "I'll Subscribe to that!"

-THE END-

UNSUBSCRIBE

A Story About One Man's
Profound Discovery

Dear Reader,

Have fun as you discover your own ways to Unsubscribe. I hope you share this effective approach with others. As you begin to Unsubscribe, I have no doubt that you will see the world around you change!

Ross Newkirk

About the Author

Ross Newkirk is an entrepreneur, inventor, and designer who has created products that make people's lives easier, and developed companies like RNventions, which sold aftermarket accessories for Jeeps. He earned a degree in Agricultural Sciences from Penn State and has fostered South American ostriches, emus, and bees. An advocate for raising human consciousness, Ross enjoys meditation, kayaking, and hiking, and lives in New Hampshire.